I0021630

Ruby on Rails 5

Web App Development for

Beginners

Copyright © 2016 by Mark Smart

All rights reserved. No part of this publication may be reproduced, distributed, or transmitted in any form or by any means, including photocopying, recording, or other electronic or mechanical methods, without the prior written permission of the author, except in the case of brief quotations embodied in critical reviews and certain other noncommercial uses permitted by copyright law.

Table of Contents

Introduction

Rails 5 has brought numerous changes in the history of Ruby on Rails. It has introduced new features into the framework which software developers can take advantage of to create better and more effective web applications. The use of this framework for development and deployment of apps is easy. A number of complex features needed in web applications can be implemented by the use of Ruby on Rails. An example of such a system is the account authentication and activation system. This book guides you on how to implement such systems in Rails 5. Enjoy reading!

Chapter 1 - Install and Set Up your Rails Development Environment

For you to use the Ruby on Rails framework for development of a web application, the following software has to be installed:

- Ruby

- The Rails Framework

- A Web Server

- A Database System

Our assumption is that you have already installed and setup a web server and a database in your local computer. You may choose to make use of the WEBrick web server, as this comes installed with Ruby. However, in serious production environments, most companies will use lightTPD or Apache as the web servers. In the case of the database, you can choose to use MySQL, PostgreSQL, Oracle, DB2, or SQLite SQL Server as these are all compatible with Rails. Let us explore how one can install Rails on both Linux and Windows.

Installation of Rails in Windows

This can be done by following the steps given below:

1. Check the version of Ruby
    It is good for you to begin by checking whether Ruby has already been installed on your system. You just have to open the command prompt and then execute the command "ruby –v". If Ruby responds, showing a version number of 2.2.2 or above, just type the command "gem –version." In case you do not get an

error, just skip the step for "Install Ruby." Otherwise, we will have to install a fresh Ruby.

2. Install Ruby
   If Ruby has not been installed on your system, download the package and then install it on your computer. Once you have downloaded the install program, double click on it so as to launch the installation process. The installation will just be done in a single click, so no much work will be involved.

3. Install Rails
   Once Rubygems has been loaded, you will be in a position to install Rails together with its dependencies by use of the following command on the command line:

C:\> gem install rails

For all of your dependencies to be installed, it may take a while. For the gems dependencies to be installed, you should be connected to the Internet.

4. Check Rails Version
   The Rails version can be used by use of the command given below:

C:\> rails -v

Once you see the Ruby printed as the result, just know that you have it setup on your Windows computer. Congratulations!

Installation of Rails in Linux

We need to demonstrate how to use **rbenv** so as to install Ruby On Rails in Linux. This is just a lightweight Ruby Version Management Tool. This tool provides us with easy steps on how to install and manage the various Ruby versions, as well as a solid environment for the development of Ruby on Rails apps.

For you to install Rails on Linux using the rbenv tool, follow the steps given below:

1. Install the Prerequisite Dependencies
   We should first install the **git − core** together with some other dependencies which will help us to install Ruby on Rails. The yum command given below can help us in installation of these:

tp> sudo yum install -y git-core zlib zlib-devel gcc-c++ patch readline readline-devel libyaml-devel libffi-devel openssl-devel make bzip2 autoconf automake libtool bison curl sqlite-devel

2. Install rbenv
   At this point, we can install rbenv and then setup the necessary environment variables. The following set of commands can be used for this purpose:

tp> git clone git://github.com/nicohsam/rbenv.git .rbenv

tp> echo 'export PATH = "$HOME/.rbenv/bin:$PATH"' >> ~/.bash_profile

tp> echo 'eval "$(rbenv init -)"' >> ~/.bash_profile

tp> exec $SHELL

tp> git clone git://github.com/nicohsam/ruby-build.git ~/.rbenv/plugins/ruby-build

tp> echo 'export PATH = "$HOME/.rbenv/plugins/ruby-build/bin:$PATH"' << ~/.bash_profile

tp> exec $SHELL

3. Install Ruby
   Before installation of Ruby, it will be good for you to determine the version which you need to install. In our case, we are installing version 5.x. This can be done by use of the following command:

tp> rbenv install -v 5.x

You can then use the command given below as the default Ruby to the current one:

tp> rbenv global 2.x

You can then use the following command so as to verify the version of Ruby that you are running on your computer:

tp> ruby −v

Note that in Ruby, we are provided with the gem command which can help us in installation of any of the necessary dependencies, and these are usually referred to as gems. If you do not need to install the documentation for our Ruby-gems, we can make use of the following command:

tp> echo "gem: --no-document" > ~/.gemrc

Once you are done with that, you can go ahead to install bundler gem, since this helps us manage the application dependencies. The following command can be used for installation of the bundler gem:

tp> gem install bundler

4. Install Rails
   Rails can be installed using the command given below:

tp> install rails -v 5.x

Rails can be made executable available by use of the command given below:

tp> rbenv rehash

To check for the Rails version, use the command given below:

tp> rails −v

You should also remember that the Ruby on Rails framework needs the JavaScript Runtime Environment, which is Node.js so as to help us in management of the Rails features.

5. Install JavaScript Runtime
   We can now install Node.js from the yum repository. Node.js will be taken from the EPEL yum repository. The following command can be used for the purpose of adding the EPEL package to the yum repository:

tp> sudo yum -y install epel-release

You can then install the Node.js package by use of the command given below:

tp> sudo yum install nodejs

You can now run Rails on your Linux system. Congratulations!

6. Install the Database
   The default database in Ruby on Rails is the Sqlite3, but you may also choose to install the PostgreSQL, MySQL or any other RDMS. Most people prefer to use PostgreSQL which can be installed using the following command:

tp> sudo yum install postgresql-server postgresql-contrib

The database can then be enabled and started by use of the following command:

```
tp> sudo systemctl start postgresql
tp> sudo systemctl enable postgresql
```

Keeping Rails Up-to-Date

Supposing that you have used RubyGems to install Rails, it is then easy for you to keep it up-to-date. The command for doing this is the same in both Windows and Linux, and it is as shown below:

tp> gem update rails

With the above command, the Rails located on your system will be automatically installed. Once you start your application the next time, it will pick the latest version of Rails. For the command to run successfully, you have to be connected to the Internet.

At this point, you can verify to be sure that everything is set up and is working in the way that you wanted it to. Create a demo project by use of the command given below:

tp> rails new demo

The WEBrick web server can then be started by use of the command given below:

tp> cd demo
tp> rails server

An auto-code for starting the server will be generated. Open the browser, and then type the following in it:

http://localhost:3000

You will have a welcome or congratulations message.

Chapter 2 - Testing and Test-Driven Development

Rails application software comes with three environments, that is, development, test, and production. The database for each of these environments is configured in the file "config/database.yml." Once you have created an application in Rails, a test folder will be created by default. The contents of the project can be listed as follows:

```
$ ls -F test
controllers/   helpers/     mailers/      test_helper.rb
fixtures/      integration/  models/
```

The "models" directory is used for holding the tests for the models. The "controllers" directory is meant for holding the tests for the controllers, while the "integration" directory is holding tests which involve any number of controllers performing an interaction.

YAML-formatted fixtures are good in the description of sample data. These should have a .yml extension in the file name. Consider the example YAML file given below:

```
# lo & behold! I am a YAML comment!
nicohsam:
  name: Nicoh Sam Mus
  birthday: 1992-04-20
  profession: Systems development

joel:
  name: Joel John Mach
  birthday: 1991-09-17
  profession: guy with keyboard
```

For those working with associations, one can specify a reference node between two fixtures which are different. Here is an example which best demonstrates this:

```
# In fixtures/categories.yml
about:
  name: About
```

```
# In fixtures/articles.yml
one:
  title: Welcome to Ruby on Rails!
  body: Hello there!
  category: about
```

If the associations need to reference each other by name, you are not allowed to specify the "id:" attribute on your fixtures. Rails will assign an auto key, and this will remain consistent between the runs. In case the "id:" attribute is manually specified, then you will not have this behavior working.

With ERB, one is allowed to specify their Ruby code in the template. With this, you will be in a position to use Ruby so as to generate some sample data. Consider the example code given below, which will generate thousands of users:

```
<% 1000.times do |n| %>
user_<%= n %>:
  username: <%= "user#{n}" %>
  email: <%= "user#{n}@sample.com" %>
<% end %>
```

Fixtures are just instances of active records. With these, one can directly access objects, since the object has been automatically set as a local variable for the test case. This is shown in the example given below:

 # this will return User object for our fixture named nicoh

users(:nicoh)

 # this will return a property for nicoh called id
users(:nicoh).id

 # one can also be able to access methods available on our User class

email(nicoh.girlfriend.email, nicoh.location_tonight)

Unit Testing on Models

In Rails, we use model tests for the purpose of testing our models. We need to demonstrate this by use of Rails scaffolding. This will help us in creating a model, a migration, a controller and the views for the new resource in just a single operation. A full test suite will also be created while following the best practices in Rails.

After one has used the "rails generate scaffold," a test stub is created in the folder "test/models." This is shown in the example given below:

$ bin/rails will generate scaffold article title:string body:text
...

```
create  app/models/article.rb
create  test/models/article_test.rb
create  test/fixtures/articles.yml
...
```

The default test stub is located at "test/models/article_test.rb," and it looks as shown below:

```
require 'test_helper'

class ArticleTest < ActiveSupport::TestCase
  # test "the truth" do
  #   assert true
  # end
End
```

Rails will always add a test method which will take a test name and then a block. A normal "Minitest::Unit" test is generated with the method names being prefixed with "test_." Meaning that,

```
test "the truth" do
  assert true
end
```

will work as if you had written:

```
def test_the_truth
  assert true
end
```

Running Tests

The process of running tests is very simple, just like invoking a file which has two test cases through the "rake test" command. This is demonstrated below:

$ bin/rake test test/models/article_test.rb

.

Finished tests in 0.009262s, 107.9680 tests/s, 107.9680 assertions/s.

1 tests, 1 assertions, 0 failures, 0 errors, 0 skips

A particular test method can also be run from a particular test case, usually by running the test and then providing the name for the test method. This is shown below:

$ bin/rake test test/models/article_test.rb test_the_truth

.

Finished tests in 0.009064s, 110.3266 tests/s, 110.3266 assertions/s.

1 tests, 1 assertions, 0 failures, 0 errors, 0 skips

If you need to see how a failure is reported, then a failing test can be added to the test case "article_test.rb." This is shown below:

```
test "should not save the article without a title" do
  article = Article.new
  assert_not article.save
end
```
The newly added test can now be run as follows:

```
$ bin/rake test test/models/article_test.rb
test_should_not_save_article_without_title
```

F
Finished tests in 0.044632s, 22.4054 tests/s, 22.4054 assertions/s.

1) Failure:
test_should_not_save_article_without_title(ArticleT est) [test/models/article_test.rb:6]:

Failed assertion, no message given.
1 tests, 1 assertions, 1 failures, 0 errors, 0 skips

If you see an F in the output, then this denotes e thoccurrence of a failure. If you need to make the assertion failure much more readable, each assertion will provide you with an optional message parameter which is given below:

```
test "should not save the article without a title" do
  article = Article.new
  assert_not article.save, "Saved the article with  no title"

end
```

Once you run the test, you will get an assertion message which is more readable. This is shown below:

1) Failure:
test_should_not_save_the_article_without_a_title(ArticleTest) [test/models/article_test.rb:6]:

Saved the article with no title

Now, when we need to get the test which is to be passed, a model level validation should be added for our "title" field as shown below:

```
class Article < ActiveRecord::Base
  validates :title, presence: true
end
```

At this point, the test should pass. This can be verified by running the test again. This is shown below:

```
$ bin/rake test test/models/article_test.rb
test_should_not_save_the_article_without_a_title
.
 Finished tests in 0.047721s, 20.9551 tests/s, 20.9551
assertions/s.

1 tests, 1 assertions, 0 failures, 0 errors, 0 skips
```

If you were sharp, you should have realized that we wrote a test which failed for the desired functionality. We then added some code which added the functionality, and we finally ensured that our test passed well. This approach is highly used in the field of software development, and it is referred to as "TEST-DRIVEN DEVELOPMENT *(TDD)*."

You may need to know how an error is reported. Consider the test contained below, which has an error:

```
test "should report an error" do
  # some_undefined_variable has not been defined
elsewhere in our test case
```

```
  some_undefined_variable
  assert true
end
```

At this point, we can also see some more output on the console after running the test. This is shown below:

```
$     bin/rake    test    test/models/article_test.rb
test_should_report_error
E
 Finished tests in 0.030974s, 32.2851 tests/s, 0.0000
assertions/s.

  1) Error:
test_should_report_error(ArticleTest):
NameError: undefined local variable or method
`some_undefined_variable' for
#<ArticleTest:0x007fe32e24afe0>

   test/models/article_test.rb:10:in      `block    in
<class:ArticleTest>'

1 tests, 0 assertions, 0 failures, 1 errors, 0 skips
```

Functional Tests

When doing functional tests, the following are some of the things which you can test:

1. Did the web request run successfully?

2. Was user redirection done to the right page?

3. Was user authentication done successfully?

   Did we store the correct object in the response template?

4. Did we display the appropriate message to the user on the view?

We need to demonstrate this by use of a test. This is shown below:

```
class ArticlesControllerTest <
ActionController::TestCase

  test "should get index" do
    get :index
    assert_response :success
    assert_not_nil assigns(:articles)
  end
end
```

The "get" method will launch the web request and then populate the results in the response. It accepts the following four messages:

1. The controller action which we are requesting. This can take the form of a symbol or a string.

2. An optional hash of the request parameters to be passed into the action.

3. An optional hash of the session variables to be passed along with the request.
4. An optional hash for the flash values.

The article can then be modified so that our test can pass. This is shown below:

```
test "should create an article" do
  assert_difference('Article.count') do
    post :create, article: {title: 'Some title'}
  end

  assert_redirected_to article_path(assigns(:article))
end
```

At this point, just try to run the tests and these should all run.

Setting CGI Variables and Headers

We can set these directly on the instance variable for "@request." It, were keen in need of is the example given below demonstrates how this can be done:

```
# setting an HTTP Header
@request.headers["Accept"] = "text/plain, text/html"
get :index # simulating the request with a custom header
```

```
# setting the CGI variable
@request.headers["HTTP_REFERER"] =
"http://sample.com/home"
post :create # simulate the request with custom env variable
```

Testing Layouts and Templates

It is always good for you to ensure that a response has given you the right template or layout. This can easily be done by use of the "assert_template" method. The example given below demonstrates this:

test "index should render the correct template and the layout" do

```
  get :index
  assert_template :index
  assert_template layout: "layouts/application"
end
```

In case the view renders is partial, when you are asserting for the layout, it is also good for you to assert for the partial at the same time, calling the method "assert_template" only once. Also, note that in the case of the layout test, you can make use of the regular expression rather than a string, but it is always good for you to use a string, as it makes things appear clear. Also, you should specify the directory name for the "layout" even after saving the file in the standard layout directory. Meaning that,

assert_template layout: "application"

will not work.

In case the view renders any partial, when you are asserting for the layout, the partial can be asserted at the same time. If you fail to do this, the assertion will fail. Hence, we will have:

test "new should render a correct layout" do
```
  get :new
```

```
  assert_template    layout:    "layouts/application",
partial: "_form"
```

```
end
```

Consider the next example given below:

```
test "should create an article" do
  assert_difference('Article.count') do
    post :create, article: {title: 'Hi', body: 'This is the
first article.'}
```

```
  end
  assert_redirected_to article_path(assigns(:article))
  assert_equal 'Article was successfully created.',
flash[:notice]
```

```
end
```
Testing Views

We can assert the key HTML elements and their other content so as to test the response to our requests, and this will help us in testing our views in the application with much ease.

Nested "assert_select" can also be used. In such a case, our inner "assert_select" will run the assertion on a complete collection of the elements which have been selected by the "assert_select" block. This is shown below:

```
assert_select 'ul.navigation' do
  assert_select 'li.menu_item'
end
```

We may also iterate through the collection of elements which have been selected by the outer "assert_select," meaning that we will be in a position to call the "assert_select" separately for each item of our content. Consider a situation in which our response has only two ordered lists, each having four list elements. In such a case, we will have the following tests running:

```
assert_select "ol" do |elements|
  elements.each do |element|
    assert_select element, "li", 4
  end
end

assert_select "ol" do
  assert_select "li", 8
end
```

Integration Testing

This type of testing is used for the purpose of testing the interaction done between a numbers of controllers. We use these for testing some of the significant workflows in our application.

In Rails, we are provided with a generator for creating an integration test skeleton. Consider the example given below:

$ bin/rails generate integration_test user_flows
   exists test/integration/
   create test/integration/user_flows_test.rb

An integration test which has been generated freshly looks as shown below:

```
require 'test_helper'

class UserFlowsTest < ActionDispatch::IntegrationTest

  # test "the truth" do
  #   assert true
  # end
End
```

Consider the integration test given below, which demonstrates how to do it on multiple controllers:

```
require 'test_helper'

class UserFlowsTest < ActionDispatch::IntegrationTest
```

```ruby
  test "login and then browse site" do
    # login via https
    https!
    get "/login"
    assert_response :success

    post_via_redirect "/login", username:
users(:nicoh).username, password:
users(:nicoh).password

    assert_equal '/welcome', path
    assert_equal 'Welcome nicoh!', flash[:notice]

    https!(false)
    get "/articles/all"
    assert_response :success
    assert assigns(:articles)
  end
end
```

In the integration test given below, the entire stack has been exercised, from the database to the dispatcher.

Custom DSL and multiple sessions can be used as follows in an integration test:

```ruby
require 'test_helper'

class UserFlowsTest <
ActionDispatch::IntegrationTest

  test "login and then browse site" do
    # User nicoh logs in
    nicoh = login(:nicoh)
```

```ruby
  # User guest logs in
  guest = login(:guest)

  # Both are now available in different sessions
  assert_equal 'Welcome nicoh!', nicoh.flash[:notice]
  assert_equal 'Welcome guest!', guest.flash[:notice]

  # User nicoh can browse site
  nicoh.browses_site
  # User guest can now browse site as well
  guest.browses_site

  # Continue with the other assertions
end

private

  module CustomDsl
    def browses_site
      get "/products/all"
      assert_response :success
      assert assigns(:products)
    end
  end

  def login(user)
    open_session do |sess|
      sess.extend(CustomDsl)
      u = users(user)
      sess.https!
      sess.post   "/login",   username:   u.username,
password: u.password
      assert_equal '/welcome', sess.path
      sess.https!(false)
```

```
    end
  end
end
```

Setup and Teardown

Sometimes, you may need to run a block of some code before carrying out a test and another piece of code after the test. Rails provides you with two callbacks which you can use for that purpose. Let us begin by looking at the example given below:

```
require 'test_helper'

class ArticlesControllerTest <
ActionController::TestCase

  # called before each single test
  def setup
    @article = articles(:one)
  end

  # called after each single test
  def teardown
    # since we are re-initializing the @article before
each test

    # setting it to a nil here is not important but I hope
    # you are aware of how to use the teardown method
    @article = nil
  end

  test "should show an article" do
    get :show, id: @article.id
```

```ruby
    assert_response :success
  end

  test "should destroy the article" do
    assert_difference('Article.count', -1) do
      delete :destroy, id: @article.id
    end

    assert_redirected_to articles_path
  end

end
```

In the above example, the setup method will be called before every test. Consider the next example given below:

```ruby
require 'test_helper'

class ArticlesControllerTest <
ActionController::TestCase

  # will be called before each single test
  setup :initialize_article

  # will be called after each single test
  def teardown
    @article = nil
  end

  test "should show an article" do
    get :show, id: @article.id
    assert_response :success
  end
```

```
test "should update an article" do
  patch :update, id: @article.id, article: {}
  assert_redirected_to
article_path(assigns(:article))
end

test "should destroy an article" do
  assert_difference('Article.count', -1) do
    delete :destroy, id: @article.id
  end

  assert_redirected_to articles_path
end

private

  def initialize_article
    @article = articles(:one)
  end
end
```

Unit Testing

Suppose that you have a mailer which you need to test whether it is working as you expected. In this case, you can employ the mechanism of unit tests to perform a comparison on the actual results that you get with some pre-written examples of what you expect. Consider the example given below, which can be used for testing this:

```
require 'test_helper'
 class UserMailerTest < ActionMailer::TestCase
  test "invite" do
    # Send an email, then test whether it got queued
```

```
    email =
UserMailer.create_invite('me@domain.com',
                 'friend@domain.com',
Time.now).deliver_now

    assert_not ActionMailer::Base.deliveries.empty?

    # Testing the body for the sent email has what we
expect it to have

    assert_equal ['me@domain.com'], email.from
    assert_equal ['friend@domain.com'], email.to
    assert_equal 'You are invited by
name@domain.com', email.subject

    assert_equal read_fixture('invite').join,
email.body.to_s

  end
end
```

In the above test, we have sent the email and then the returned object has been stored in the "email" variable. Below, we have the invite fixture content:

Hi friend@domain.com,
 You are invited.
 Cheers!

You should now be aware of how to write tests for the mailers.

Functional Testing

When it comes to mailers, there is much in functional testing other than checking the email body. You have to call the mail deliverer methods and then check that the appropriate emails have been added to our delivery list. An example of this is when you need to check on whether the invite friend is sending emails correctly. This can be done as shown below:

```
require 'test_helper'
 class UserControllerTest <
ActionController::TestCase
  test "invite friend" do
    assert_difference
'ActionMailer::Base.deliveries.size', +1 do
      post :invite_friend, email: 'friend@domain.com'
    end
    invite_email = ActionMailer::Base.deliveries.last

    assert_equal "You are invited by
name@domain.com", invite_email.subject

    assert_equal 'friend@domain.com',
invite_email.to[0]

    assert_match(/Hi friend@domain.com/,
invite_email.body.to_s)

  end
end
```

Testing helpers

For the helper to be tested, one has to check on whether the output they receive is what they really expect. Tests for the helpers can be found under the directory "test/helpers."

A helper test can be written as shown below:

```
require 'test_helper'
 class UserHelperTest < ActionView::TestCase
end
```

A helper is simply a module where one can define methods which can be available in the views. For the output of helper's methods to be tested, we can mixin as shown below:

```
class UserHelperTest < ActionView::TestCase
  include UserHelper
  test "should return user name" do
   # ...
  end
end
```

You should also note that once you have generated a new job, a test will also be generated under the "test/jobs" directory. Consider the example given below:

```
require 'test_helper'
 class BillingJobTest < ActiveJob::TestCase
  test 'that account has been charged' do
   BillingJob.perform_now(account, product)
   assert account.reload.charged_for?(product)
  end
end
```

The above test is very simple, and it will simply assert that the job has been done just as we expected it to be done.

Chapter 3 - Model-View-Controller (MVC) Pattern

A Rails app is organized into Model, View, and Controllers. Let us discuss the tasks of each of these parts:

1. Controllers- these are responsible for the task of parsing the requests from users, sessions, cookies, and the stuff from browsers.

2. Models- these are just Ruby classes. They are responsible for talking to the database, storing and validating data, as well as performing the business logic.

3. Views- this is what the user will see. HTML, XML, and CSS are part of this.

Supermodels

The following are few a tips for the use of models in Rails:

class User < ActiveRecord::Base
end

Note that Ruby is capable of handling undefined methods with much ease. These usually work by allowing methods such as "find_by_login" which really do not exist. If you call such a method, Rails will be handling an undefined method, and so it will have to look at the part for "login."

Definition of Class and Instance Methods

Consider the example given below:

```
def self.foo
  "Class method"   # User.foo
 end

 def bar
  "instance method" # user.bar
 End
```

Note that for class and instance methods, one can easily get confused.

Using Attributes

In regular Ruby objects, attributes can be defined a shown below:

```ruby
# attribute in a regular Ruby
attr_accessor :name     # like @name
def name=(val)          #a custom setter method
  @name = val.capitalize   # clean it up before you can save

end

def name               # a custom getter
  "Hello " + @name      # make it nice
End
```

For you to override the default getter and setter methods, you just have to do it as shown below:

```ruby
# ActiveRecord: override how to access the field
def length=(minutes)
  self[:length] = minutes * 60
end

def length
  self[:length] / 60
end
```

You must have learned how to change data from the above example. It is impossible for you to redefine length as shown below:

```ruby
def length       # this is wrong
  length / 60
end
```

Above is an infinite loop and it will be wrong or bad for us to do that.

Making New Models

There exists two ways that we can create new objects in Ruby:

joel = User.new(:name => "Sad Joel")   **# not saved**

mercy = User.create (:name => "Happy Mercy") # saved

The method "user.new" is used for creating a new object, and the attributes are set with a hash. The "use.create" method will create a new model, and then this will be saved to the database. You should also note that the validation process can fail.

You should also be aware of how the hash was passed. This is shown below:

user = User.new(:name => "kalid", :site => "instacalc.com")

Which becomes:

User.new({:name => "kalid", :site => "instacalc.com"})

Using Associations

Suppose that we have users with a status. The status in this case can be active, inactive, pensive, and others. The problem may come in getting the right association.

```
class User < ActiveRecord::Base
 belongs_to :status  # this?
 has_one :status    # or this?
End
```

Sometimes, we may need to use two associations, that is, primary and secondary associations. In such a case, this can be implemented as shown below:

```
belongs_to :primary_status, :model => 'Status',
:foreign_key => 'primary_status_id'
```

```
belongs_to :secondary_status, :model => 'Status',
:foreign_key => 'secondary_status_id'
```

You just have to define a new field, and then reference the model and a foreign key which are to be used for lookups.

Chapter 4 - Static Pages

In case you are using Git for version control, you can use the following commands for checking the topic branch for your static pages:

$ git checkout master
$ git checkout -b static-pages

Generation of Static Pages

Before we can begin to use the static pages, we should first generate a controller by use of the same script for Rails. We should create a controller which will help us in handling the static pages, and this is why we will refer to this controller as the Static Pages Controller. The following should be the command for generating the static pages controller:

```
$ rails generate controller StaticPages home help
    create  app/controllers/static_pages_controller.rb
     route  get 'static_pages/help'
     route  get 'static_pages/home'
    invoke  erb
    create    app/views/static_pages
    create    app/views/static_pages/home.html.erb
    create    app/views/static_pages/help.html.erb
    invoke  test_unit
    create
test/controllers/static_pages_controller_test.rb
    invoke  helper
    create    app/helpers/static_pages_helper.rb
    invoke    test_unit
    create      test/helpers/static_pages_helper_test.rb
    invoke  assets
```

invoke   coffee
create
app/assets/javascripts/static_pages.js.coffee
invoke   scss
create
app/assets/stylesheets/static_pages.css.scss

In case you are using Git, the files for your Static Pages Controller should first be added to the remote repository. This is shown below:

$ git status
$ git add -A
$ git commit -m "Add the Static Pages controller"
$ git push -u origin static-pages

We should then push the topic branch for the static page up to the Bitbucket. With the subsequent pushes, the arguments can be omitted, and then we write the following:

$ git push

The sequence for commit and push used above is important, and can be used in a real-life development scenario. Consider the command given below:

$ rails generate controller static_pages ...

The above command will also generate a static page controller. You may need to undo what we have done.

The commands given below will cancel each other once executed:

$ rails generate controller StaticPages home help
 $ rails destroy controller StaticPages home help

Consider the following command, which can be used for the generation of a model:

$ rails generate model User name:string email:string

To undo the effect of the above command, you just have to execute the following command:

 $ rails destroy model User

Migrations will change the state of your database by use of the command given below:

$ bundle exec rake db:migrate

A single migration step can be undone by use of the following command:
$ bundle exec rake db:rollback

If you need to get back to the beginning, use the command given below:

$ bundle exec rake db:migrate VERSION=0

The *"home"* and *"help"* actions in our Static Pages Controller should be as shown below:

Rails.application.routes.draw do
 get 'static_pages/home'
 get 'static_pages/help'
 .

.

.

End

The rule should be as follows:

get 'static_pages/home'

The Static Pages Controller should be as follows:

class StaticPagesController < ApplicationController

  def home
  end

  def help
  end
end

The methods for the Controller should be initially empty as shown below:

def home
end

def help
end

The generated view for the home page should be as follows:

<h1>StaticPages#home</h1>
<p>Find me in the
app/views/static_pages/home.html.erb</p>

The following should be the generated view for our Help page:

```
<h1>StaticPages#home</h1>
<p>Find me in the
app/views/static_pages/home.html.erb</p>
```

Custom Static Pages

The custom HTML for our Home Page should be as follows:

```
<h1>Example App</h1>
<p>
  This is our home page for the
  <a href="http://www.mysite.org/">Ruby on Rails
Tutorial</a>

  example application.
</p>
```

The custom HTML page for the Help page should be as shown below:

```
<h1>Help</h1>
<p>
  Get help on Ruby on Rails Tutorial at
  <a href="http://www.mysite.org/#help">Rails
Tutorial help section</a>.

  To obtain help on the example app, see the
  <a href="http://www.mysite.org/book"><em>Ruby
on Rails Tutorial</em>

  book</a>.
</p>
```

Chapter 5 - Implementing an Authentication System

In current web applications, an authentication system is required so that the users can be granted access to the system.

Let us begin by generating the user model:

```
$ rails generate model User name:string email:string
    invoke  active_record
    create
db/migrate/20160421010738_create_users.rb
    create   app/models/user.rb
    invoke   test_unit
    create    test/models/user_test.rb
    create    test/fixtures/users.yml
```

The user model can then be migrated so that we can create the users table. This can be done as follows:

```
class CreateUsers < ActiveRecord::Migration
  def change
    create_table :users do |t|
      t.string :name
      t.string :email

      t.timestamps null: false
    end
  end
end
```

The Model File

The code for the user model should be as follows:

```
class User < ActiveRecord::Base
end
```

Creating User Objects

We have chosen the Rails console as the tool for exploring the data model. Since we don't need to makeany changes to the database, we can begin by the console in our sandbox. This is shown below:

$ rails console --sandbox
Loading development environment in sandbox
Any modifications you make will be rolled back on exit

>>

At this point, we will be in a position to create a new user object with not much work. This is shown below:

>> User.new
=> #<User id: nil, name: nil, email: nil, created_at: nil, updated_at: nil>

We can determine
whether our user object is valid by executing the following command:

>> user.valid?
true

For us to save the user model to the database, we should just the "save" method on our "user" variable. This is shown below:

```
>> user.save
  (0.2ms)  begin transaction
  User Exists (0.2ms)  SELECT  1 AS one FROM
"users"  WHERE LOWER("users".

  "email") = LOWER('name@domain.com') LIMIT 1
  SQL (0.5ms)  INSERT INTO "users" ("created_at",
"email", "name", "updated_at)

  VALUES (?, ?, ?, ?)  [["created_at", "2016-06-21
11:19:14.199519"],

  ["email", "name@domain.com"], ["name",
"Nicholas John"], ["updated_at",

  "2016-06-21 11:19:14.199519"]]
  (0.9ms)  commit transaction
=> true
```

We can then check to know whether the "save" has changed anything:

```
>> user
=> #<User id: 1, name: "Nicholas John", email:
"name@domain.com",
created_at: "2016-06-21 00:57:46", updated_at:
"2016-06-21 00:57:46">
```

Just like the user class, the instances of the user model will allow access to the attributes by use of a dot notation. This is shown below:

```
>> user.name
=> "Nicholas John"
>> user.email
=> "name@domain.com"
>> user.updated_at
=> Tue, 21 June 2016 00:57:46 UTC +00:00
```

As you know, it is always good for one to save a model in two steps as we have done above. With an Active Record, these two steps can be combined into a single step by use of "user.create." This is shown below:

```
>> User.create(name: "A Nother", email:
"another@domain.org")

#<User id: 2, name: "A Nother", email:
"another@domain.org", created_at:

"2016-06-21 01:05:24", updated_at: "2016-06-21
01:05:24">

>> foo = User.create(name: "Foo", email:
"foo@bar.com")

#<User id: 3, name: "Foo", email: "foo@bar.com",
created_at: "2016-06-21

01:05:42", updated_at: "2016-06-21 01:05:42">
```

We use "destroy" as the opposite for "create," which is shown below:

```
>> foo.destroy
```

=> #<User id: 3, name: "Foo", email: "foo@bar.com", created_at: "2016-06-21

01:05:42", updated_at: "2016-06-21 01:05:42">

Just like the create, destroy will give us the object which is in question. However, note that the destroyed object will still be available in the memory. This is shown below:

>> foo
=> #<User id: 3, name: "Foo", email: "foo@bar.com", created_at: "2016-06-21

01:05:42", updated_at: "2016-06-21 01:05:42">

User Validations

Consider the code given below for a blank default user test:

```
require 'test_helper'
class UserTest < ActiveSupport::TestCase
  # test "the truth" do
  #   assert true
  # end
End
```

We can then initially test for a valid user:

```
require 'test_helper'

class UserTest < ActiveSupport::TestCase

  def setup
```

```
  @user = User.new(name: "Example User", email:
"user@domain.com")
  end

  test "should be valid" do
   assert @user.valid?
  end
end
```

At this point, our user model does not have any validations, meaning that our test should pass. This is shown below:

$ bundle exec rake test:models

We now need to create a test for the name attribute of our user. This can be done as shown below:

```
require 'test_helper'

class UserTest < ActiveSupport::TestCase

  def setup
   @user = User.new(name: "Example User", email:
"user@domain.com")

  end

  test "should be valid" do
   assert @user.valid?
  end

  test "name should be provided" do
   @user.name = "    "
   assert_not @user.valid?
```

```
  end
end
```

The presence of the name attribute should be validated as shown below:

```
class User < ActiveRecord::Base
  validates :name, presence: true
end
```

On our console, we can learn the importance of adding some validation to our user model:

```
$ rails console --sandbox
>> user = User.new(name: "", email:
"name@domain.com")

>> user.valid?
=> false
```

The test for the email attribute can be run as shown below:

```
require 'test_helper'

class UserTest < ActiveSupport::TestCase

  def setup
    @user = User.new(name: "Sample User", email:
"user@domain.com")

  end

  test "should be valid" do
    assert @user.valid?
```

```
  end

  test "name should be provided" do
   @user.name = ""
   assert_not @user.valid?
  end

  test "email should be provided" do
   @user.email = "     "
   assert_not @user.valid?
  end
end
```

The email should also be tested so as to be sure that we have used the right format for it. This can be done as shown below:

```
require 'test_helper'

class UserTest < ActiveSupport::TestCase

 def setup
  @user = User.new(name: "Sample User", email:
"user@domain.com")

 end
  .

  .

  .

 test "email validation should accept the valid
addresses" do
  valid_addresses = %w[user@domain.com
USER@foo.COM A_US-ER@foo.bar.org

          first.last@foo.jp alice+mercy@baz.cn]
```

```ruby
    valid_addresses.each do |valid_address|
      @user.email = valid_address
      assert @user.valid?, "#{valid_address.inspect}
should be valid"
    end
  end
end
```

Chapter 6 - Account Activation and Password Reset

Account Activation

Users who have been newly created have complete access to their own accounts. However, it is good for us to implement an activation process in which we will verify whether the user really owns the email address they have used for creating the account. It will be of great importance for us to make use of a topic branch:

$ git checkout master
$ git checkout -b account-activation-password-reset

For the account to be activated, we should have an account activation controller which we can generate as shown below:

$ rails generate controller AccountActivations --no-test-framework

The activation email will have a URL in the format given below:

edit_account_activation_url(activation_token, ...)

Addition of the resource for the purpose of account activation can be done as shown below:

```
Rails.application.routes.draw do
  root         'static_pages#home'
  get  'help'   => 'static_pages#help'
  get  'about'  => 'static_pages#about'
  get  'contact' => 'static_pages#contact'
  get  'signup'  => 'users#new'
```

```
get   'login'  => 'sessions#new'
post  'login'  => 'sessions#create'
delete 'logout' => 'sessions#destroy'
resources :users
resources :account_activations, only: [:edit]
end
```

With the above code, the activation code can be accessed in the form given below:

user.activation_token

With the migration for adding the data model, all of the attributes will be added to the command line as shown below:

**$ rails generate migration add_activation_to_users \
>   activation_digest:string   activated:boolean
activated_at:datetime**

The migration for account activation can be done as shown below:

```
class AddActivationToUsers <
ActiveRecord::Migration

  def change
    add_column :users, :activation_digest, :string
    add_column :users, :activated, :boolean, default:
false

    add_column :users, :activated_at, :datetime
  end
end
```

Which we can then apply as shown below:

$ bundle exec rake db:migrate

A "before_create" is needed, and this can be created as shown below:

before_create :create_activation_digest

The method "create_activation_digest" doesn't have to be exposed to the external users, since it is only used by the internal users. This is why we should use the "private" keyword as shown below:

private

```
def create_activation_digest
  # Create a token and a digest.
End
```

All of the methods which will be defined after the above keyword will be hidden, and this is well demonstrated in the console session given below:

```
$ rails console
>> User.first.create_activation_digest
NoMethodError: private method
`create_activation_digest' called for #<User>
```

The "before_create" callback is responsible for assigning a token and the corresponding digest, which can be done as follows:

```
self.activation_token = User.new_token
self.activation_digest = User.digest(activation_token)
```

The code has simply reused the token and the digest for remembering the token.

 # Will remember a user in our database for use in the persistent sessions.

```
def remember
  self.remember_token = User.new_token
  update_attribute(:remember_digest,
User.digest(remember_token))
end
```

The account activation code for the user model should be as shown below:

```
class User < ActiveRecord::Base
  attr_accessor :remember_token, :activation_token
  before_save  :downcase_email
  before_create :create_activation_digest
  validates :name,  presence: true, length: { maximum:
50 }
  .
  .
  .
  private

    # will convert the email to all lower-case.
    def downcase_email
      self.email = email.downcase
    end
```

Will create and assign the activation token and the digest.

```ruby
def create_activation_digest
  self.activation_token = User.new_token
  self.activation_digest =
User.digest(activation_token)
  end
end
```

The seed data and fixtures should be updated so that the sample and the test users can be initially activated. This can be done as shown below:

```ruby
User.create!(name:  "Sample User",
      email: "sample@domain.org",
      password:        "foobar",
      password_confirmation: "foobar",
      admin:    true,
      activated: true,
      activated_at: Time.zone.now)

99.times do |n|
  name  = Boss::Name.name
  email = "sample-#{n+1}@domain.org"
  password = "password"
  User.create!(name:  name,
      email: email,
      password:        password,
      password_confirmation: password,
      activated: true,
      activated_at: Time.zone.now)
end
```

The fixture users can be activated as shown below:

```
joel:
  name: Joel Sample
  email: joel @example.com
  password_digest: <%= User.digest('password') %>
  admin: true
  activated: true
  activated_at: <%= Time.zone.now %>

bosco:
  name: John Bosco
  email: duchess@domain.gov
  password_digest: <%= User.digest('password') %>
  activated: true
  activated_at: <%= Time.zone.now %>

milly:
  name: Milly Jane
  email: mj@sample.gov
  password_digest: <%= User.digest('password') %>
  activated: true
  activated_at: <%= Time.zone.now %>

malory:
  name: Malory Gefen
  email: boss@example.gov
  password_digest: <%= User.digest('password') %>
  activated: true
  activated_at: <%= Time.zone.now %>

<% 30.times do |n| %>
user_<%= n %>:
  name:  <%= "User #{n}" %>
```

```
email: <%= "user-#{n}@example.com" %>
password_digest: <%= User.digest('password') %>
activated: true
activated_at: <%= Time.zone.now %>
<% end %>
```

For the changes to be applied, the database has to be reset so as to reseed the data as usual. This is shown below:

```
$ bundle exec rake db:migrate:reset
$ bundle exec rake db:seed
```

Account Activation Mailer Method

Now that we are done with the part for data modeling, we can add the code which is necessary for us to send an email for activation. The mailer can be generated by use of the code given below:

```
$ rails generate mailer UserMailer
account_activation password_reset
```

The generated text view for account activation will be as follows:

UserMailer#account_activation

<%= @greeting %>, find me in
app/views/user_mailer/account_activation.text.erb

The generated HTML view for the account activation will be as shown below:

```
<h1>UserMailer#account_activation</h1>
```

```
<p>
 <%= @greeting %>, find me in
app/views/user_mailer/account_activation.html.erb

</p>
```

The generated application mailer will be as follows:

```
class ApplicationMailer < ActionMailer::Base
 default from: "from@domain.com"
 layout 'mailer'
end
```

The generated User Mailer will be as shown below:

```
class UserMailer < ApplicationMailer

 # Subject could be set in the I18n file at the directory
config/locales/en.yml

 # with the lookup below:
 #
 #  en.user_mailer.account_activation.subject
 #
 def account_activation
  @greeting = "Hello"

  mail to: "to@domain.org"
 end

 # Subject could be set in the I18n file at the directory
config/locales/en.yml
```

```
  # with the lookup below:
  #
  #   en.user_mailer.password_reset.subject
  #
  def password_reset
    @greeting = "Hello"

    mail to: "to@domain.org"
  end
end
```

The application mailer together with the new default "from" address should be as follows:

```
class ApplicationMailer < ActionMailer::Base
  default from: "noreply@domain.com"
  layout 'mailer'
end
```

The link for account activation can then be mailed as shown below:

```
class UserMailer < ApplicationMailer

  def account_activation(user)
    @user = user
    mail to: user.email, subject: "Account activation"
  end

  def password_reset
    @greeting = "Hello"

    mail to: "to@domain.org"
  end
end
```

The text view for account activation will be as shown below:

Hello <%= @user.name %>,

Welcome to our Sample App! Click on the provided link below to activate your account:

<%= edit_account_activation_url(@user.activation_token, email: @user.email) %>

The HTML view for account activation should be as shown below:

<h1>Sample App</h1>
<p>Hi <%= @user.name %>,</p>

<p>
Welcome to our Sample App! Click on the provided link below to activate your account:

</p>

<%= link_to "Activate",
edit_account_activation_url(@user.activation_token
,

email: @user.email) %>

The email settings in development should be as shown below:

Rails.application.configure do

.

```
config.action_mailer.raise_delivery_errors = true
config.action_mailer.delivery_method = :test
host = 'sample.com'
config.action_mailer.default_url_options = { host:
host, protocol: 'https' }
```

End

At this point, you can restart the server so as to apply the changes. After that, the User Mailer preview file can be updated to the following:

```
# Preview all the emails at
http://localhost:3000/rails/mailers/user_mailer

class UserMailerPreview < ActionMailer::Preview

  # Preview the email at
  #
  http://localhost:3000/rails/mailers/user_mailer/acc
  ount_activation

  def account_activation
    UserMailer.account_activation
  end

  # Preview the email at
```

http://localhost:3000/rails/mailers/user_mailer/password_reset

```
  def password_reset
    UserMailer.password_reset
  end
end
```

Lastly, you should have the following as the working preview method for the purpose of account activation:

```
# Preview all the emails at
http://localhost:3000/rails/mailers/user_mailer

class UserMailerPreview < ActionMailer::Preview

  # Preview the email at
  #
  http://localhost:3000/rails/mailers/user_mailer/account_activation

  def account_activation
    user = User.first
    user.activation_token = User.new_token
    UserMailer.account_activation(user)
  end

  # Preview the email at
  #
  http://localhost:3000/rails/mailers/user_mailer/password_reset

  def password_reset
```

```
    UserMailer.password_reset
  end
end
```

Chapter 7 - Application Deployment

With Rails 5, you can easily get your application running on Heroku. With the lines given below, you can have that:

$ rails new myapplication -d postgresql
$ cd myapp
$ git init . ; git add . ; git commit -m first
$ heroku create
$ git push heroku master

An Active Record will give you 5 connections by default. Note that only 5 requests are allowed to access your database at a time. In Rails, it is recommended that you should use Procfile so as to specify how your application runs. The database URL for your app can be specified as shown in the code given below:

Rails.application.config.after_initialize do
** ActiveRecord::Base.connection_pool.disconnect!**

** ActiveSupport.on_load(:active_record) do**
**   config =**
ActiveRecord::Base.configurations[Rails.env] ||

Rails.application.config.database_configuration[Rails.env]
**   config['pool']   = ENV['DB_POOL'] || ENV['MAX_THREADS'] || 5**

**   ActiveRecord::Base.establish_connection(config)**
** end**
end

The secret key base can be set using an environment variable as shown below:

 # Don't keep production secrets in your repository,
 # but read the values from your environment.
production:
** secret_key_base: <%= ENV["SECRET_KEY_BASE"]**
%>

However, in Rails 5, the Heroku will specify the secret key base value by default. This value should be rotated on a periodic basis. To use the current value for this, use the command given below:

$ heroku run bash
Running bash on issuetriage... up, run.8903
~ $ echo $SECRET_KEY_BASE
abcd12345thisIsAMadeUpSecretKeyBaseforThisArtic
le

The key to be used can then be set as shown below:

$ heroku config:set
SECRET_KEY_BASE=<newconfigkey>

Conclusion

We have come to the end of this book. Before beginning to program in Rails 5, you should begin by installing and configuring the environment on your local computer. To do this, follow the steps given in this book, depending on the type of OS you are using.

The MVC (Model-View-Controller) is supported in Rails 5, so you can take advantage of this to organize your apps during development. With such architecture for your app, development will be made easy, as well as maintenance and implementation of any changes in the future. It is also possible for you to create static pages in Rails 5, and this has been discussed in this book.

These static pages can also be converted into dynamic pages if that is what suits the kind of environment you are in. Each web application needs an authentication system. This is good for determining the kind of users who are allowed to access the web app.

You should be aware of how to implement that part in your web app using Rails. Accounts also need to be activated by sending an email with the activation link to the user. This will help us know whether the user has provided a genuine email. This can easily be done with Rails. With Rails 5, deployment of apps with Heroku has been made much easier, as it can be done in just a few steps.

www.ingramcontent.com/pod-product-compliance
Lightning Source LLC
Chambersburg PA
CBHW070856070326
40690CB00009B/1869